META-ANALYSIS MADE EASY

How to Draw Definitive Conclusions from Inconclusive Studies and Find Untapped Gold Mines for Further Research!

PAUL D. ELLIS

Meta-Analysis Made Easy:
How to Draw Definitive Conclusions from Inconclusive Studies and
Find Untapped Opportunities for Further Research!

ISBN: 978-1-927230-58-9
Copyright © 2020 by Paul Ellis

Published by MadMethods, an imprint of KingsPress.org,
PO Box 66145, Beach Haven, Auckland 0749, New Zealand. To
get this title in other formats and to find other titles in the
MadMethods series, visit www.MadMethods.co

Version: 1.1 (September 2020)

Dedication: For my colleagues.

What are readers saying about
The Essential Guide to Effect Sizes?

I cannot agree with reviewers who say this book is just for beginners. I think it is brilliant for everyone who wants to conduct meta-analysis. It is a very easy way to start thinking meta-analytically. Highly recommended!

— Amazon Reviewer

A wonderful resource! I have read many books on research and statistical methods but few that convey the concepts as clearly as this one, and fewer still that I can say I actually enjoyed reading. I would recommend it to those who are just starting to grapple with research methods as well as the more experienced researcher.

— Carrington Shepherd

Easy to read, understand, and follow. If you want to know more about meta-analysis and effect sizes, this is the book for you!

— Amazon Reviewer

Excellent book that clearly explains the concepts behind statistical mechanics. Easy to read.

— John Frias Morales

Meta-analyses have become incredibly important over the last 30 years or so. This book is a good read, not at all heavy on technical jargon or formulas. This text is a good review text for anyone in graduate school who is conducting a study or writing a thesis for possible publication. Good information, well-written, and informative. Heartily recommended. Five stars.

— John V. Karavitis

An easy read on a complex topic. Great resource!
— Amazon Reviewer

"Scientists have known for centuries that a single study will not resolve a major issue. Indeed, a small sample study will not even resolve a minor issue. Thus, the foundation of science is the cumulation of knowledge from the results of many studies."

— Hunter and Schmidt (1990: 13)

Contents

Why do I need this book?

This is a book for those preparing to start research projects. Whether you are a doctoral candidate or a full-chair professor, you may be asking questions like: How do I draw conclusions from inconclusive studies? How can I identify fruitful avenues for further research? How big a sample do I need to have a fair chance of detecting the effects I am seeking? This book will provide you with the tools you need to start answering these sorts of questions.

If you are a quantitative researcher, it's essential that you know something about meta-analysis. Now you could spend $80 on some brick of a book that contains more Greek than English and which you'll never read, or you could read this jargon-free introduction. You could sign up for a few classes, or you could spend an hour reading this book.

The examples in this book have been proven in the field and the classroom. They work. If you need to know about meta-analysis in a hurry, you won't find a better starting point.

Five reasons to read this book

There are at least five reasons why quantitative researchers should be familiar with meta-analysis:

1. Meta-analyses, in contrast with traditional narrative summaries or literature reviews, can bring order to a large and disparate set of studies. Meta-analyses are a powerful tool for establishing evidentiary benchmarks, even when prior research has been inconclusive.

2. A meta-analysis informs research by providing estimates of effect size that are essential to prospective analyses of statistical power. Want to know how many subjects you need for your own study? A meta-analysis of past research gives you the best estimates of effect size.

3. Effect size estimates generated by meta-analyses provide nonzero benchmarks against which research results can be compared. Meta-analysis thus provides researchers with more informed interpretation scenarios than merely assessing the likelihood of a null hypothesis.

4. A well-designed meta-analysis can examine contextual and other moderators that could not be easily tested in an individual study. The assessment of moderator effects is a powerful feature of meta-analysis as it can lead to new and unexpected discoveries.

5. Perhaps the most intriguing feature of meta-analysis is the process can lead to new hypotheses and promote theory development. Meta-analysis should not be seen as the culmination of past research, but as a doorway to further avenues of enquiry.

Who wrote this book?

I'm the inventor of meta-analysis. Actually, I'm not. Not by a long shot. But for a few weeks I thought I was.

I'm kind of embarrassed to admit this, but for a short time in my life I thought I had discovered meta-analysis. It happened about twenty years ago while attending a conference in Murcia, Spain. It was a warm afternoon and my mind drifting towards a siesta. I was thinking about effect sizes when I was struck by a bolt of lightning. "If we pooled effect size estimates from different studies, we could come up with an average estimate that was more accurate than any of the individual estimates."

Eureka! The opportunity was so obvious, I couldn't believe no one had thought of this before.

"What's more, we could weigh each estimate by the quality of the study from which it was obtained." It was a genius idea. If there was a Nobel Prize for research methods, I was going to get it!

Sadly, my euphoria lasted just as long as it took to learn of Gene Glass and Mary Lee Smith. Turns out Glass and Smith had beaten me by 30 years.

Although no one knows exactly who first came up with the idea of meta-analysis, Glass and Smith are widely acknowledged as pioneers for their seminal study of psychotherapy treatments (Glass 1976; Smith and Glass 1977). Wanting to know whether psychotherapy is beneficial, Glass and Smith set out to collect all the available evidence. They analyzed 833 effects obtained from 375 studies and found that psychotherapy works. This was great news for psychologists, but even better news was their novel technique of quantitatively pooling and analyzing the results of past research.

Glass and Smith's meta-analytic innovation sparked a revolution. In no time at all, meta-analyses were being used to examine all sorts of unresolved issues, particularly in the field of psychology. Meta-analysis had arrived.

I came to the party late, but better late than never. Learning how to think meta-analytically completely changed the way I looked at past research. I now had a tool far superior to the standard lit. review. I couldn't wait to try my hand at my first meta-analysis.

I was both thrilled to discover meta-analysis and saddened that I hadn't learned this stuff sooner. None of my methods teachers had said anything about it. I scanned the methods books on my shelves. The texts that did mention meta-analysis struck me as un-necessarily dense and hard to read.

Rather than curse the darkness I decided to light a candle. I wrote my own textbook, *The Essential Guide to Effect Sizes: Statistical Power, Meta-Analysis, and the Interpretation of Research Results*. It's a comprehensive yet jargon-free introduction to the largely ignored subject of effect sizes and their role in meta- and statistical power analyses.

When my book came out, I set up a website called www.effectsizefaq.com. The site has helpful tips and tricks along with links to useful resources. The site has proven popular with researchers attracting millions of page views.

By monitoring traffic stats, I have discovered that researchers and students are looking for straight-forward answers to three important questions:

(1) What is an effect size?
(2) How do I calculate the statistical power of my study?
(3) How do I draw definitive conclusions from inconclusive studies?

The book you are reading answers the third question. Two other books in the MadMethods series, *Effect Size Matters* and *Statistical Power Trip*, answer the first and second questions respectively. If you are unfamiliar with the concept of effect sizes, I recommend reading the first book before diving into this one. A good understanding of effect sizes and how to measure them is an essential precursor to meta-analysis. And if you wish to learn how to use effect sizes to design studies with sufficient power to detect them, the second book shows you how. (Value tip: You get three-books-in-one for a low price in the omnibus version.)

Why did I write these little books when I have already written a perfectly good text? Because students are poor and researchers are busy. You probably don't have six months to come to grips with these new subjects. You just want the short version. Your attitude is, *Just show me how!*

Your wish is granted.

This book is a quick and easy introduction to the subject of meta-analysis. By the time you're done reading it, you should be able to conduct a basic meta-analysis and recognize some of the pitfalls that undermine them.

Paul D. Ellis

Two ways to summarize past research

Research is cumulative in nature. At least, it's meant to be. But how often have you read the literature on a certain topic and come away scratching your head? "Study A reported a strong link between X and Y, Study B said there was no link, and Study C said the link ran in the opposite direction."

What do you do with disparate results? You conclude that a lack of consensus indicates a need for further research, so you do your own study. You get a result similar to Study C. "Hooray. My study found the same thing as that study. Progress!" But you can't help wondering what to do with the contrary results of Studies A and B.

Ideally, the results from different studies ought to line up. With each replication, we should be increasingly confident of the generalizability of emerging findings. But often what happens is the researcher is faced with the daunting task of making sense of disparate results.

This happened to me when I was a young researcher. At the time, I was interested in the relationship between market orientation and business performance. Is there one? You would expect so. Firms that are customer oriented ought to perform better, right? I surveyed the literature and what I found is summarized in Table 1.

Table 1: Market orientation research

Date	Country	Finding
1990	USA	strong
1993	USA	strong
1993	UK	weak
1995	UK	none
1995	New Zealand	none
1996	USA	strong
1998	Hong Kong	weak
2000	Korea	weak
2000	Germany	strong
2001	Australia	moderate
2001	India	strong

The beautiful thing about this body of work, is there is a lot of research measuring a common relationship or effect. The annoying thing is the results don't converge. Some studies say market orientation has a strong effect on performance; others say there is no effect. Which is it? Does market orientation affect performance or doesn't it? Why, after all this work, do we not have a straight answer to this question?

The fault lies not in the research, but in my summary of it. On what basis did I decide some results were strong, weak, or non-existent? It also appears that I gave every study equal weight, but was this fair? Surely a result drawn from a large sample deserves more weight than a result drawn from a small one, but I made no such distinction.

And herein lies the problem with the standard literature review, a.k.a., the narrative review.

What's wrong with narrative reviews?

There are two ways to review past research; a qualitative approach, also known as a narrative review, and a quantitative approach, also known as meta-analysis. Most PhD students and junior academics are familiar with the first approach. When beginning a study they collect all the relevant research, and then they try to make sense of it. They might attempt a short summary of past results. "Study A found this. Study B found that." Or they might create a table like the one above. In either case, definitive conclusions will be hard to draw because narrative summaries suffer from several inherent failings. First, they provide only a broad-brushed survey of extant work. Past results may be classified as "strong" or "weak" but what makes them so? Who decides? If a study reported a non-result, was that because there was no effect to detect or because the study lacked the power to detect it?

Second, narrative reviews typically fail to discriminate between studies done well and those done poorly. What are we to do with outlier studies? Do we treat them the same? Do we pretend we didn't see them? And what makes a study an outlier anyway?

Worst of all, narrative summaries are prone to researcher bias. How can we be sure the researcher has surveyed the entire field? Have they included unpublished studies? Were they thorough? And what have they done with awkward or contrary findings? Were they honest?

Reviewing past research is essential if we are to circumscribe the boundaries of existing knowledge and avoiding repeating past mistakes. But qualitative summaries of extant work are inherently limited. A far superior approach is to evaluate research using a quantitative approach or meta-analysis.

What is meta-analysis?

Meta-analysis is the statistical analysis of statistical analyses. Meta-analysis combines and compares the findings of different studies such that each study comprises an independent observation in the final sample of effect sizes.

Meta-analysis is quantitative in the sense that each study in the sample contributes a number, namely, a study-specific estimate of the effect size. We are not interested in whether the study's authors thought their results were strong or weak. They can keep their conclusions. We just want to see their evidence.

You may be wondering about effect sizes. An effect is simply an outcome, a result, a reaction, or a change in Y brought about by a change in X. An effect size refers to the magnitude of an outcome as it occurs, or would be found, in nature or in a population.

For instance, you may be interested in the effect of a vaccine on an infectious disease, or a policy change on presidential approval ratings, or a new strain of cereal on crop yields. An effect exists, or doesn't exist, out there, in the real world. When a scientist looks for evidence of the effect in a sample, they end up with an *estimate* of the effect size.

The estimate is the thing.

An effect size estimate will be more or less accurate depending on a variety of factors. How well was it measured? How representative was the sample? That sort of thing. The job of the scientist is to accurately estimate the size of the effect. In contrast, the job of the meta-analyst is to combine all the estimates obtained in different studies to come up with an average estimate. If the meta-analyst does their job well, their weighted mean estimate will be an accurate estimate of the true effect size.

I hope you are beginning to understand the value of a good meta-analysis. While a narrative review may leave you with more questions than answers, a good meta-analysis will deliver a very precise answer to the question everyone has been searching for, namely, *how big is the effect size?*

Why meta-analysis rocks

The chief attraction of meta-analysis is that it offers a framework for a scientifically rigorous accumulation of extant research findings. By doing meta-analysis we hope to identify the conclusions that would've been reached had the data from all the independent studies been collected in one big study.

When I "discovered" meta-analysis, I felt like I had found a gold mine. That's because my field, international business, is one big mess of studies done on a variety of topics in a variety of settings using a variety of methods. Before meta-analysis, I saw the mess; after meta-analysis, I saw unlimited opportunity. I will tell you about my first meta-analysis, and the surprising results it generated, below. But first, we need to ask…

What are the ingredients for good meta-analysis?

You have collected all the relevant research on a particular topic, and you want to summarize the results. You know narrative reviews tend to be flawed. Can you run a meta-analysis instead? It depends.

Not every body of work is amenable to meta-analysis. Meta-analysis requires that findings must be both (a) conceptually comparable and configured in (b) statistically equivalent forms (Lipsey and Wilson 2001).

Are the studies in your sample measuring essentially the same thing in essentially the same way? Or are they comparing apples with oranges?

In the market orientation example I gave you earlier, I neglected to mention that there are two ways to measure market orientation. Because two tools were devised by different authors at around the same time, the research can be divided into two groups depending on which tool they used; tool 1 or tool 2. Does this mean we cannot combine the results of these studies? Not necessarily.

In fact, the use of different measures can provide the meta-analyst with a unique opportunity to compare the effect of different measurement procedures. We'll return to this point below.

The second requirement for meta-analysis is the findings must be statistically equivalent. Is it possible to determine a common measure of effect size across studies? How do we compare studies that variously report t-tests, Chi-square, correlations, path coefficients, phi-coefficients, etc.? If studies report results in different metrics, the only way we can compare the results is by converting them all into a common measure of effect size.[1]

If the research you wish to review meets these two requirements of being conceptually comparable and statistically equivalent, you can conduct meta-analysis.

---

[1] Some procedures for doing this are covered in my MadMethods book *Effect Size Matters*.

How to bake a cake: meta-analysis in 4 easy steps

A while ago I began a graduate methods class with a question. "How many of you have done a meta-analysis."

No hands went up.

"How many of you believe you will have completed your first meta-analysis before our class is done?" A few uncertain hands went up, but most stayed down.

Meta-analysis sounds hard but it's actually straightforward. It's like baking cake. As long as you stick to the recipe, you'll end up with something good.

Let me prove this by using the example I use in the classroom.

To keep things simple, let's imagine we are interested in a body of research consisting of four studies (see Table 2).

Table 2: Four fictitious studies

	Study 1	Study 2	Study 3	Study 4
r	0.453	0.321	0.301	0.075
p	<0.001	0.049	0.033	0.722
n	87	38	50	25

Here we have four studies each reporting estimates of an effect size in the correlational metric. (The numbers in this example come from Field (1999).) Three of the studies reported a statistically significant result ($p < .05$), but one did not. However, we care nothing for these p-values. They are irrelevant to our meta-analysis. We are primarily interested in the individual effect size estimates (r) and the sample sizes (N) from which they were obtained.

The primary purpose of a meta-analysis is to calculate an estimate of the population effect size based on the individual sample-based estimates. The easiest way to do that is to average the correlations.

Summing the correlations in Table 1 and dividing by the number of samples (four) gives an average r of 0.288. This is our mean effect size, and the first thing we notice about it is that it is appreciably lower than three of the four observed correlation coefficients.

This demonstrates how the simple average can be biased.

In our dataset, a very small correlation coefficient was reported in Study 4. Although this estimate came from a small sample, it was given equal weight with the estimates obtained from larger samples. This is hardly ideal and it probably compromised our result. Why? Because larger samples return better effect size estimates than smaller ones.

One solution to this problem is to calculate a weighted average using this formula from Hunter and Schmidt (1990):

$$\bar{r} = \frac{\sum n_i r_i}{\sum n_i}$$

The Greek letter sigma means sum. (I promise you this is one of the few times any Greek symbols will appear in this book!) We multiply each study's effect size estimate (r) by the sample size (n), sum the lot, then divide the result by the sum of the four sample sizes. This gives us a weighted mean effect size (or r-bar) as follows:

$$= \frac{(87 \times 0.453) + (38 \times 0.321) + (50 \times 0.301) + (25 \times 0.075)}{87 + 38 + 50 + 25}$$

$$= \frac{68.53}{200}$$

$$= 0.343$$

The weighted mean effect size (0.343) is larger than the unweighted one (0.288). Is this a better estimate of the population effect size? Most definitely. By giving more weight to the larger samples, we have reduced the contaminating effects of sampling error.

But wait, there's more!

The effect size estimates returned in each study are also affected by the reliability or internal consistency of the measures used. Studies reporting low measurement reliability generate estimates that are lower than the true or population effect size on account of noisy measures.

So let us introduce one more piece of information into the analysis. Cronbach's alpha (α) is routinely reported in studies measuring variables with multi-item scales. In Table 3 below, the alpha obtained from each study is reported in the second to last row.

Table 3: Four corrected effect sizes

	Study 1	Study 2	Study 3	Study 4
r	0.453	0.321	0.301	0.075
n	87	38	50	25
α	0.94	0.70	-	0.82
Corrected ES	*0.467*	*0.384*	*0.332*	*0.083*

We correct for measurement error by dividing each effect size (r) by the square root of the reliability of the measurement instrument (α). For studies failing to report reliabilities, such as Study 3, we substitute the mean reliability observed across the whole dataset. Crunching the numbers gives the corrected effect sizes we see in the bottom row of Table 3. Plugging these into the same equation above gives us a weighted mean effect size corrected for measurement error, as follows:

$$= \frac{(87 \times 0.467) + (38 \times 0.384) + (50 \times 0.332) + (25 \times 0.083)}{87 + 38 + 50 + 25}$$

$$= \frac{73.90}{200}$$

$$= 0.369$$

Because we have pooled the results of past research, we can be reasonably confident that our weighted mean effect size of $r = 0.369$ is closer to the true population effect size, than any of the estimates obtained in the four individual studies.

Which is pretty cool.

If you have managed to follow along—it wasn't that hard, was it?—congratulations! You've just learned how to do a meta-analysis.

Actually, you have learned how to do one type of meta-analysis. There are several meta-analytic methods, but two dominate. The Coke and Pepsi of meta-analysis, if you like, are the rival methods developed by Hunter and Schmidt (2000) and by Hedges (1981, 2007). The method we have just learned is the Hunter and Schmidt method. If you would like to learn about the others, check out any good meta-analysis textbook. And if you would like more practice on crunching the numbers, check out the exercises in the Appendix.

Now that you've learned how to do a basic meta-analytic procedures, let me illustrate the process using an example based on my first published meta-analysis (Ellis, 2006). In my meta-analysis, I was interested in the effect of a market orientation on performance. In the business literature, there is a large body of research that says being customer focused and so forth either has a strong effect or no effect on business performance. A narrative review of this research will give you no clear conclusion, but can a meta-analysis do better?

To answer this question, I followed four steps:

(i)   compile a set of effect size estimates
(ii)   calculate a weighted mean effect size
(iii)   calculate a confidence interval for the mean effect size
(iv)   interpret the results

Step 1: Compile a set of effect sizes

Remember, a meta-analysis can only be done on research that is conceptually comparable and statistically equivalent. Market orientation research fits both criteria as it is a well-defined body of work examining the same relationship (the effect of market orientation on performance) with results usually reported in the correlational metric.

While a narrative review may be selective, a good meta-analysis ought to be thorough. Every estimate of the effect size should be included. In my case, I began by conducting a census of all the relevant research. I systematically searched databases relevant to my field for empirical articles published from 1990 to 2004, and I manually scanned published references.

My initial search yielded 202 journal articles plus four soon-to-be-published studies. I was so dazzled by the large number of studies I had found, that I made my first mistake. I did not consider *unpublished* studies. Full disclosure: This means my analysis may have been compromised by the availability bias. More on this in Part B.

My starting point (the 206 papers) led me to identify a smaller number of independent studies. To be included in my meta-analysis, each study had to report a sample size and some measure of effect size. Since most of the studies in my database reported a correlational measure of effect size, I adopted r as the effect size of interest. If a study did not report zero-order correlations or provide statistics which could be converted to a correlation, I wrote to the authors to solicit correlations directly.

(Tip for scholars: In your descriptive stats, always report your correlation matrix. Even if your results are statistically nonsignificant, meta-analysts will want to see them.)

You don't need a special statistical program to conduct a meta-analysis. A well laid-out spreadsheet will suffice. In my spreadsheet, each row corresponded to a single study, while each column contained quantitative details about the studies. From each study I recorded the effect size, the sample size, and the type of tool used to measure market orientation. I also recorded the reliability of the measurement tool (Cronbach's alpha), and the type of performance variables reported. I also recorded some contextual information about each study, such as where it was done.

In my study, the outcome or dependent variable was performance. Performance can be a tricky beast to measure. In my dataset a variety of measures had been adopted and it was important to take these differences into account. Consequently, I coded studies according to the scope of their performance measure (i.e., business-level measures such as profits or market-specific measures such as customer satisfaction) and the type of measures used (i.e., objective versus subjective assessments).

Any study that reported an effect size more than 2.5 standard deviations from the combined mean was considered an outlier and dropped from the meta-analysis. (One study was deleted.) When I was done compiling my dataset, I had 58 useable studies. Collectively these studies reported data collected from 14,586 firms based in 28 different countries.

Step 2: Calculate a weighted mean effect size

At the end of Step 1, I had a set of 58 effect size estimates, drawn from different studies. However, these estimates were not directly comparable on account of differences in sample size and measurement reliability. To attenuate the effects of sampling and measurement error, effect size estimates were divided by the square root of the reliability of the measurement instrument and weighted by the size of the sample from which they were obtained. For studies failing to report reliabilities, a mean reliability figure was substituted.

After correcting for sample size and measurement error, I was able to calculate a weighted mean effect size of $r = 0.26$. (It's a simple number, but it represents a lot of work.) What does my result mean? While narrative summaries of past research give ambiguous conclusions, examining the effect sizes directly leads to the unequivocal conclusion that market orientation is positively related to business performance, just as you would expect.

So far, so good. But can we say more? And how confident are we that our estimate of the effect size is close to the true effect size? To answer that question, I needed to...

Step 3: Calculate the confidence interval for the weighted mean

The end result of a meta-analysis is a single estimate of the population effect size. (That doesn't sound like much, but you can do a lot with that number as we will see in Part B.) How do we know if our estimate—the weighted mean—is any good?

To answer that question, we can convert the result to a z score then determine whether the probability of obtaining a score of this size is less than .05, or we can calculate a 95 percent confidence interval. In meta-analysis, the latter approach is more common.

A confidence interval establishes the degree of precision in the estimate of the mean effect size. Unlike a standard test of statistical significance, confidence intervals are centered on observed values rather than the hypothetical value of a null hypothesis.

With a confidence interval, we are looking for two things. First, does the range of the interval include 0? A 95% confidence interval that excludes 0 puts the odds of $p = 0$ beyond reasonable possibility and indicates that the mean effect size is statistically significant at $\alpha = .05$.

Second, is the interval narrow or wide? Narrow is better and more precise. Confidence intervals will be wider for distributions that are heterogeneous, that is, where two or more population means have been combined into a single estimate of mean effect size.

To calculate a confidence interval for a mean effect size, we need to know the standard error (SE) or (v_r) variance of the mean effect size. This can be found by multiplying the square of the difference between each effect size estimate and the mean by the sample size, summing the lot, then dividing the result by the total sample size. Hunter and Schmidt (1990) provide the equation:

$$v_{\cdot_r} = \frac{\sum n_i (r_i - \bar{r})^2}{\sum n_i}$$

In my market orientation study the variance or SE was 0.0087. To calculate the upper and lower bounds of my confidence interval, I multiplied the SE by the critical value of the z-distribution (1.96 when $\alpha = .05$), then subtracted (or added) the result to the mean effect size (0.263) to determine the lower (or upper) bounds of the confidence interval:

$$\text{Confidence interval} = \bar{r} \pm 1.96 SE_{\bar{r}}$$

Doing this gave me a CI95 of 0.246−0.280. Since this range excluded zero, I concluded that my result was statistically significant.

Step 4: Interpret the results

The final step in any analysis is to interpret the results. We do this by asking, what do the results mean and for whom? If Step 3 tells us whether a result is statistically significant, then Step 4 is concerned with the practical or substantive significance of the result.

Once upon a time, any meta-analysis that was done well stood a decent chance of getting published. Provided you did a fair job collecting and coding studies, knew how to crunch the numbers, you'd get a hit. Those days are long gone. Now editors expect more. Consider the following advice which comes from the editor of the prestigious *Academy of Management Journal*:

> AMJ will publish meta-analyses that fulfil the promise of the method's champions: advancing theoretical knowledge. A meta-analysis that merely tallies the existing literature quantitatively but provides no new insights into the nature of the relationships so tallied will not be favored. A meta-analysis that sheds new light on how or why a relationship or set of relationships occurs should be (re)viewed favorably. (Eden 2002: 844)

Identifying the contribution to theory is just one part of the interpretation challenge. Increasingly, editors want answer to questions like these: Are the results reported in non-arbitrary metrics that can be understood by nonspecialists? What is the context of this effect? Who is affected or who potentially could be affected by this result and why does it matter? What is the net contribution to knowledge? Does this result confirm or disconfirm what was already known or suspected? Is this result small, medium, or large?

I discuss the interpretation challenge in my MadMethods book *Effect Size Matters*, and I won't repeat that material here. However, it is worth noting that meta-analyses offer unique interpretation opportunities. The meta-analyst, with her big picture of the data, can see things that were missed in the individual studies. How meta-analysis leads to the discovery of new knowledge is the subject of Part B.

Intermission

In Part A our focus was on the pooling of effect size estimates from prior research. One of the reasons we collect and combine these estimates is to delineate the boundaries of existing knowledge. Another reason is to identify potentially interesting avenues for further exploration.

If the question in Part A was, "what do we know?" the question we now turn to in Part B is, "where do we go from here?"

Meta-analysis and the discovery of new knowledge

A good meta-analysis represents more than the culmination of a stream of research and is a stepping stone to new and exciting avenues of research and theory development.

Meta-analysis contributes to theory by making sense of the literature and by examining the influence of contextual moderators.

What is a moderator?

A moderator is a third variable that affects or moderates the relationship between an X and Y. In my market orientation meta-analysis, I examined a number of measurement- and contextual-moderators.

Recall that there are two ways or tools for measuring market orientation. By coding studies on the basis of which tool they used, I was able to assess whether the choice of measurement tool had any effect on the central relationship.

It did.[2]

And since there are different ways of measuring performance, I was able to test for that as well. Specifically, I coded tests based on whether they assessed performance using objective or subjective measures. Crunching the numbers revealed market orientation had a stronger correlation with the latter.

Measurement moderators are interesting in that they inform prospective analyses of statistical power and steer future researchers towards particular measurement tools, but where meta-analysis really shines is in the analysis of contextual moderators.

My meta-analysis was based on 58 separate studies conducted in 28 different countries. This offered me a unique opportunity to see whether effect sizes were affected by things like economic development and culture. Essentially, I wanted to know whether the

------

[2] If you're a business researcher, you may be interested to learn that studies measuring market orientation using items inspired by Kohli, Jaworski and Kumar's (1993) MARKOR scale returned significantly higher effect sizes (r = .32, CI = .29 – .36) than those inspired by Narver and Slater's (1990) MKTOR instrument (r = .25, CI = .23 – .27).

market orientation—performance relationship is universal or whether it's affected by local market conditions. I had good reasons for suspecting the effect of a market orientation might be ameliorated by the sort of country you live in.

Consider two businesses that are equally market oriented. Both are highly focused on their customers and competitors. However, the first business is located in a free market economy characterized by buyers' markets and intense competition, while the second is located in a developing economy characterized by sellers' markets and rapid growth. Do these location differences affect the potency of each firm's market orientation?

That's what I wanted to find out.

To do this I coded each study according to a number of contextual or country-specific variables. These included the cultural distance from the U.S., and the size and economic development of the home economy at the time of data collection. (If you want to know how I quantified these variables, see Ellis (2006).)

I won't bore you with the details, but my findings confirmed my suspicion that effect sizes were larger when measured in mature, western markets, and relatively small in underdeveloped economies that are culturally distant from the US (see Table 4).

Table 4: Mean effect sizes for moderator sub-groups in Ellis (2006)

Contextual moderators		n	Corrected r	95% CI
Culture	West	37	0.285	0.262 - 0.307
	East	19	0.228	0.201 - 0.255
Cultural dist.	Low	28	0.286	0.262 - 0.309
from U.S.	High	29	0.236	0.212 - 0.261
Market size	Small	29	0.222	0.200 - 0.244
	Large	29	0.322	0.295 - 0.348
Economic	Developing	28	0.228	0.206 - 0.251
development	Mature	30	0.308	0.282 - 0.333

For an international business researcher, this was an intriguing finding, pregnant with possibilities. But here's the thing: this discovery was made without collecting any primary data.

If I had designed a multi-country study to search for these effects, it would have been prohibitively expensive. (Fourteen thousand firms in 28 countries!) But obtaining this knowledge required nothing more than access to prior research, an Excel spreadsheet, and a little meta-analytic thinking.

How to ruin
a meta-analysis

If you've come this far, you may be thinking "Meta-analyses are awesome," and you're not wrong. But like any tool, they can be abused and misused.

Now that I have impressed you with the story of my first meta-analysis, it's time to 'fess up and tell you what I got wrong. Although it wasn't a bad first attempt, in hindsight I could have done some things better.

There are several ways to scuttle a meta-analysis, but the greatest danger may be that presented by the exclusion of relevant research.[3] By design, a meta-analyst will seek to include all estimates of an effect size in their study. To the degree that some estimates are missed, the meta-analytic results may be compromised by an availability bias.

---

[3] Other sources of bias, which I cover in *The Essential Guide to Effect Sizes*, are the inclusion of false results, the use of inappropriate statistical models, and running meta-analyses with insufficient statistical power.

What is an availability bias?

An availability bias arises when effect size estimates obtained from studies which are readily available (e.g., published studies, conference papers) differ from those obtained from studies which are less accessible (e.g., unpublished studies, studies written in foreign languages).

I said that running a meta-analysis is as easy as baking a cake. It is, provided you have all the ingredients. A more accurate analogy might be to say that meta-analysis is like baking a cake when some of the ingredients are hard to find. Miss key ingredients and you could ruin your cake.

Imagine ten scientists all investigating the same effect. Five of them get statistically significant results and go on to publish their findings. However, the other five scientists leave their nonsignificant results filed away and unpublished. What can we say about these ten studies?

All things being equal, the five published studies probably found larger effect sizes than the unpublished ones. This happens because statistical significance is determined by several variables, one of which is the effect size. Since journals are in the habit of publishing studies that found something as opposed to studies that found nothing, studies which find larger effects are more likely to get published than studies which find smaller ones. And this is bad news for meta-analysts.

Actually, it's bad news for everyone.

When results don't pan out, research goes unreported. "I didn't get a good p-value. No editor will want to see this." No editor won't, but a meta-analyst will.

Your carefully conducted study contains a legitimate estimate of an effect size and that will always be of interest to other researchers, regardless of the results of statistical significance tests.

An availability bias can emerge in a variety of ways. The first source of an availability bias is the so-called **file drawer problem** which arises when researchers do nothing with their results. Got an unexpected or nonsignificant result? Don't hide it. Report it. If you can't get it in a journal, present it as a conference paper. At the very least, put it on your website and make it publicly available.

Related to the file drawer problem is the **reporting bias** which arises when researchers only report some of their findings.

Say you run four tests and get two statistically significant results. If you only publish the two "good" results while filing away the others, you will inadvertently contribute to an availability bias and the inflation in effect sizes obtained in subsequent meta-analyses. Again, this happens because statistical significance is related to effect size. Small effects are less likely to generate statistically significant results. But this doesn't mean they're invalid, useless, or wrong. In the right context, small effects can be profoundly important.

In addition to researchers, editors also limit the availability of research if they exhibit a preference for publishing statistically significant results. A **publication bias** emerges when statistically nonsignificant results obtained from methodologically sound studies lead to the nonpublication of those studies.

There is considerable evidence that this happens in practice (Coursol and Wagner, 1986). What does this mean for the meta-analyst? Base your study exclusively on published research, and you will likely end up with inflated estimates of the effect size.

Finally, there is the wonderfully-named **Tower of Babel bias** whereby results published in languages other than English are excluded from meta-analyses. There is research to show that non-native English speakers are more likely to submit to English-language journals when their results are "strong," meaning big and statistically significant, and are less likely to do so when their results are less impressive (Grégoire *et al.*, 1995).

How to deal with an availability bias?

A good meta-analysis will include every estimate of a particular effect size, regardless of whether the estimate is small or large, positive or negative, published or filed away. But the presence of an availability bias undermines this goal.

What can the meta-analyst do? Obviously, they need to make every effort to collect those estimates. Getting estimates from published research is easy; getting estimates which have gone unreported or have been filed away is tricky.

A good meta-analyst will put out calls on discussion boards and research groups. They will reach out to scholars known to be working in the area. They may not be able to collect every unreported result, but even some will be better than none.

A meta-analyst who succeeds in collecting unpublished results can compare the mean estimates obtained from those results with those obtained from published results. This will enable them to quantify and mitigate the threat of the availability bias.

Another remedy is to calculate the "fail-safe N." The fail-safe N is the number of additional studies with contrary evidence (e.g., null results) that would be needed to overturn a meta-analytic conclusion. The aim is to make the fail-safe N as high as possible. The higher the N the more confidence we have in the meta-analysis.

Another way to quantify the threat of an availability bias is to create a funnel plot showing the distribution of effect sizes. A funnel plot is a scatter plot where each effect size estimate is placed on a XY graph where X corresponds to the effect size and Y corresponds to the sample size. The idea is that the precision of the estimates increases with sample size.

Relatively imprecise estimates obtained from small samples will be scattered widely along the bottom of the graph, while more precise estimates obtained from larger samples will be in a tighter bunch at the top of the graph. If you have collected a representative database of effect sizes, the dispersion of results will describe a funnel shape. However, the existence of an availability bias will render the plot asymmetrical.

I mentioned earlier than in my market orientation meta-analysis, I collected results from published studies and conference papers. I did not make any effort to collect unpublished results because it never occurred to me to do so. Hindsight is a wonderful thing. If I had been aware of the threat of an availability bias, I could have done something about it.

Better late than never. Figure 1 is a funnel plot I created specifically for this book. Each dot on the plot represents a study-specific estimate of the effect size, while the diamond represents the weighted mean obtained across the fifteen studies in this group. To reduce clutter, the plot only contains the subset of studies that used the first tool for measuring market orientation.

Figure 1: Funnel plot for Ellis (2006)

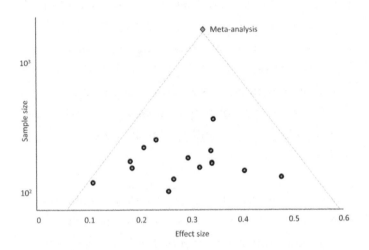

Does the scatterplot in Figure 1 appear symmetrical and funnel-shaped? It generally does. The widest spread of results appears along the bottom while results from larger studies are more closely bunched together at the top. This is what we would expect to see if there was little threat from an availability bias.

If we were being picky, we might argue that there is a bit of vacant space towards the lower right side of the funnel. But this space would have been occupied by studies returning large effect sizes, while the presence of an availability bias would suggest an absence of studies returning small ones.

No funnel plot is perfect, and mine is about as good as they come. Consequently, I can be reasonably confident that my dataset was not compromised by an availability bias.

Phew!

Enough about me and my brilliant meta-analysis. It's time to discuss someone else's meta-analysis, and this one is a doozy.

Meta-analysis and moon madness

Is mental health affected by the moon? It seems a strange question, but moon madness, has long been the stuff of folklore. (Have you ever noticed how the word *lunacy* derives from *luna*, the Latin word for moon?) Sceptics scoff at the association, but serious research has examined links between phases of the moon and various types of undesirable behaviour.

Scholars who subscribe to the "lunar effect" suspect that there may be an element of truth behind folk beliefs or that the beliefs create self-fulfilling prophecies. In either case, a number of hypotheses have been advanced to explore lunar-lunacy links: variations in moonlight may affect the pineal gland triggering unusual behaviour; criminals may prefer the darkness provided by a new moon; bodily fluids may be affected by the moon's gravitational pull, and so on.

Needless to say this work is considered highly controversial among psychologists. On the one side are those who argue that any positive findings are examples of Type I error, while on the other side are those who argue that failures to observe any lunar effect are examples of Type II error and under-powered research.

To settle this issue, Rotton and Kelly (1985) conducted a meta-analysis of 37 published studies investigating links between phases of the moon and outcomes such as homicides, suicides, psychiatric disturbances, admissions to mental institutions, and calls to crisis centers.

Interestingly, they found some statistically significant, though very small effects. However, they reasoned that these results may have been upwardly biased by a file drawer problem that is probably greater for lunar research than other fields of enquiry. If 100 scientists decided to test the lunar hypothesis and one happened to find a result, that particular scientist would be far more likely to get his paper published than the 99 who found nothing.

Rotton and Kelly also rejected a causal link on conceptual grounds arguing that the lunar hypothesis consistently fails the tests of replicability and predictability.

> Just as we cannot prove that werewolves, unicorns and other interesting creatures do not exist, we cannot prove that the moon does not influence behavior. However, the burden of proof lies with those who favour the lunar hypothesis. They will have to collect a great deal more—and better—data before they can reject the null hypothesis of no relation between phases of the moon and behaviour. (1985: 300)

The moon madness study highlights the overarching importance of careful interpretation. Rotton and Kelly found *something*—their meta-analysis detected some effects—but concluded their something was really nothing given the high likelihood of a large and confounding availability bias. Meta-analysis is a useful tool, but in science, replication is everything.

Thinking meta-analytically

Now that you have a basic grasp of the issues, you may be inspired to attempt a meta-analysis of your own. Go for it! But start by investing in a good text book. Although we have peeled away some of the mystery surrounding meta-analysis, this short guide should not be considered a substitute for comprehensive text.

If you have no interest in attempting a meta-analysis, hopefully you have at least learned the value of thinking meta-analytically. If so, you will no longer be swayed by authors' conclusions or vague statements of significance. When reading empirical literature, your mindset will be, "Show me the evidence, and let me decide for myself."

And thus we come full circle. To think meta-analytically requires some expectations regarding effect sizes and the ability to analyze statistical power. Like the legs on a stool, these three concepts are intimately related.

Author's note

If you enjoyed *Meta-Analysis Made Easy*, would you mind posting a short customer review on Amazon? Doing so will help others find this book.

Thank you!

Appendix: Bonus exercise

In my graduate methods class, I would give students three papers to read for the purposes of completing a simple meta-analysis. If you would like to try this exercise for yourself, the papers are (1) Langerak *et al.*, (2004), (2) Slater and Narver (2000), and (3) Selnes *et al.*, (1996).

- Task 1: Skim read the papers to fill in the gaps in the table below (sample size, Cronbach's alpha for the market orientation instrument (α), effect size (r), and corrected effect size)
- Task 2: Calculate a simple mean effect size
- Task 3: Calculate a weighted mean effect size
- Task 4: Calculate a weighted mean effect size corrected for measurement error

The answers are found on the following page.

Study	Setting	N	MO α	r	Perf.	Corrected ES
1	Netherlands				Org. perf.	
2	USA				ROI	
3a	Scandinavia				Subj. perf.	
3b	USA				Subj. perf.	

Answers to the exercise:

Task 1: Complete the table

Study	Sample N	MO α	r	Perf.	Corrected ES
1	126	0.84	0.33	Org. perf.	0.360
2	53 (SBUs)	0.77	0.362	ROI	0.413
3a	237 (SBUs)	0.89	0.21	Subj. perf.	0.223
3b	222 (SBUs)	0.89	0.34	Subj. perf.	0.360

Task 2: Calculate a simple mean effect size

$$\frac{0.33 + 0.362 + 0.21 + 0.34}{4} = 0.31$$

How do you feel about this result? Does it seem accurate?

In this simple approach, all studies are treated equally. But notice how the largest correlation was reported in the smallest study, while the smallest correlation was found in the largest sample.

Let us attenuate our mean effect size by weighting each correlation by the sample size on which it is based.

Task 3: Calculate Weighted Mean Effect Size

$$= \frac{(126 \times 0.33) + (53 \times 0.362) + (237 \times 0.21) + (222 \times 0.34)}{126 + 53 + 237 + 222}$$

$$= \frac{(41.58) + (19.19) + (49.77) + (75.48)}{638}$$

$$= 0.29$$

Task 4: Calculate Weighted Mean Corrected for Measurement Error

Redo Task 3 above using estimates of effect size that have been corrected for measurement error.

$$= \frac{(126 \times 0.36) + (53 \times 0.413) + (237 \times 0.223) + (222 \times 0.36)}{126 + 53 + 237 + 222}$$

$$= \frac{(45.36) + (21.89) + (52.85) + (79.92)}{638}$$

$$= 0.314$$

References

Coursol, A. and E.E. Wagner (1986), "Effect of positive findings on submission and acceptance rates: A note on meta-analysis bias," *Professional Psychology: Research and Practice,* 17(2): 136-137.

Eden, D. (2002), "Replication, meta-analysis, scientific progress, and *AMJ*'s publication policy," *Academy of Management Journal,* 45(5): 841–846.

Ellis, P.D. (2006), "Market orientation and performance: A meta-analysis and cross-national comparisons," *Journal of Management Studies,* 43(5): 1089–1107.

Field, A.P. (1999), "A bluffer's guide to meta-analysis I: Correlations," *Newsletter of the Mathematical, Statistical and computing section of the British Psychological Society,* 7 (1), 16–25.

Grégoire, G., F. Derderian, and J. LeLorier (1995), "Selecting the language of the publications included in a meta-analysis: Is there a Tower of Babel bias?" *Journal of Clinical Epidemiology,* 48(1): 159-163.

Glass, G. (1976), "Primary, secondary, and meta-analysis of research," *Educational Researcher* 5:3–8.

Hedges, L.V. (1981), "Distribution theory for Glass's estimator of effect size and related estimators," *Journal of Educational Statistics,* 6(2): 106–128.

Hedges, L.V. (2007), "Meta-analysis," in C.R. Rao and

S. Sinharay (2007), *Handbook of Statistics, Vol.26,* Amsterdam: Elsevier, 919–953.

Hunter, J.E. and F.L. Schmidt (1990) *Methods of Meta-Analysis,* Newbury Park, CA: Sage.

Hunter, J.E. and F.L. Schmidt (2000), "Fixed effects vs. random effects meta-analysis models: Implications for cumulative research knowledge," *International Journal of Selection and Assessment,* 8(4): 275–292.

Kohli, A.K., B.J. Jaworski and A. Kumar (1993), "MARKOR: A measure of market orientation," *Journal of Marketing Research,* 30 (November): 467-477.

Langerak, F., E.J. Hultink, and H.S.J. Robben (2004), "The impact of market orientation, product advantage and launch proficiency on new product performance and organizational performance," *The Journal of Product Innovation Management,* 21(2): 79-94.

Lipsey, M.W. and D.B. Wilson (2001) *Practical Meta-Analysis,* Thousand Oaks, CA: Sage.

Narver, J.C. and S.F. Slater (1990), "The effect of a market orientation on business profitability," *Journal of Marketing,* 54 (October): 20-35.

Rotton, J. and I.W. Kelly (1985), "Much ado about the full moon: A meta-analysis of lunar-lunacy research," *Psychological Bulletin,* 97(2): 286–306.

Selnes, F., B.J. Jaworski, and A.K. Kohli (1996), "Market orientation in United States and Scandinavian companies," *Scandinavian Journal of Management*, 12(2): 139-157.

Slater, S.F. and J.C. Narver (2000), "The positive effect of a market orientation on business profitability: A balanced replication," *Journal of Business Research*, 48(1): 69-73.

Smith, M.L. and G.V. Glass (1977), "Meta-analysis of psychotherapy outcome studies," *American Psychologist*, 32(9): 752–760.

Made in the USA
Monee, IL
11 November 2020